Questions, Answers & Explanations

EASA PPL Revision Papers

Principles of Flight

Written and illustrated by
Helena B A Hughes

POOLEYS
Air Pilot Publishing

Nothing in this manual supersedes any EU legislation, rules or EASA regulations or procedures and any operational documents issued by The Stationery Office, the Civil Aviation Authority, National Aviation Authorities, the manufacturers of aircraft, engines and systems, or by the operators of aircraft throughout the world. Note that as maps and charts are changed regularly, those extracts reproduced in this book must not be used for flight planning or flight operations.

Copyright © 2017 Pooleys Flight Equipment Limited.

EASA Private Pilot Licence Aeroplane Questions, Answers & Explanations – Principles of Flight

ISBN 978-1-84336-207-4

First Edition published February 2014
Reprinted June 2014
Reprint October 2015
Reprint February 2016
Reprint January 2017

Origination by Pooleys Flight Equipment Limited.

Published by Pooleys Flight Equipment Ltd

Elstree Aerodrome
Hertfordshire WD6 3AW
Tel: +44(0)20 8953 4870
Web: www.pooleys.com
Email: sales@pooleys.com

AUTHOR

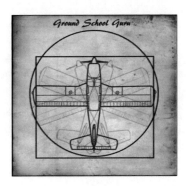

Helena B A Hughes

Helena Hughes was born into an aviation household, having her first informal "flying lesson" at the age of four. Her late father David was a flying instructor and also flew corporate jets. On leaving University Helena obtained her PPL. Shortly afterwards she started work in Air Traffic Control at London Luton Airport earning her Controllers Licence in 1990. Helena continues to be an operational Air Traffic Control Officer and is currently posted to Swanwick working "Thames Radar", "Luton Radar" and "Heathrow Special"; she is involved in controller training as both an Instructor and Assessor. Helena holds a fixed wing CPL/IR and has been a flying instructor since 1996. She also holds a PPL(H) and is a Radio Telephony and Air/Ground Examiner.

Helena would like to thank: Mrs. Brenda "Bedda" Hughes; Mr. Andrew Temple of Solent Flight Ltd; A Vrancken and H Ewing

INTRODUCTION

This book is intended as an aid to revision and examination preparation for those studying for the grant of an EASA PPL. Ideally its use should follow a period of self or directed study to consolidate the knowledge acquired and identify any areas of weakness prior to attempting the PPL examinations themselves.

The questions and answers in this publication are designed to reflect those appearing in the current examination papers and are set out in a representative format. No attempt has been made to replicate any actual examination paper.

Blank answer sheets are provided at the end of the book which may be photocopied to enable multiple attempts at each exam.

EDITORS

Dorothy Saul-Pooley LLB(Hons) FRAeS

Dorothy holds an ATPL (A) and a CPL (H), and is both an instructor and examiner on aeroplanes and an instructor on helicopters. She is Head of Training for a school dedicated to running Flight Instructor courses at Shoreham. She is also a CAA Flight Instructor Examiner. In addition, having qualified as a solicitor in 1982, Dorothy acted for many years as a consultant specialising in aviation and insurance liability issues, and has lectured widely on air law and insurance issues. This highly unusual combination of qualifications led to her appointment as Honorary Solicitor to the Guild of Air Pilots and Navigators (GAPAN). Dorothy is a Fellow of the Royal Aeronautical Society, first Chairman of the GAPAN Instructor Committee, and past Chairman of the Education & Training Committee. She has just completed her term of office as the Master for the year 2014-15 of the Honourable Company of Air Pilots (formerly GAPAN). She is also Chairman of the Professional Flying Instructors Association. In 2003 she was awarded the Jean Lennox Bird Trophy for her contribution to aviation and support of Women in Aviation and the BWPA (British Women Pilots Association). In 2013 Dorothy was awarded the prestigious Master Air Pilots Certificate by GAPAN. A regular contributor to seminars, conferences and aviation publications. Dorothy is the author and editor of a number of flying training books and has published articles in legal and insurance journals.

Daljeet Gill BA(Hons)

Daljeet is the Head of Design & Development for Pooleys Flight Equipment and editor of the Air Pilot's Manuals, Guides to the EASA IR & CPL Flight Test, Pre-flight Briefing and R/T Communications as well as many other publications. Daljeet has been involved with the editing, typesetting and designing of all Pooleys publications and products since she joined us in 2001. Graduating in 1999 with a BA(Hons) in Graphic Design, she deals with marketing, advertising, exhibition design and technical design of our manufactured products in the UK. She maintains our website and produces our Pooleys Catalogue. Daljeet's design skills and imaginative approach have brought a new level of clarity and readability to the projects she has touched.

Sebastian Pooley FRIN MRAeS

Sebastian is Managing Director of Pooleys Flight Equipment and a Director of Air Pilot Publishing. He holds a PPL (A). Sebastian is a Committee Member of the GANG - the General Aviation Navigation Group, part of the Royal Institute of Navigation and a judge for the International Dawn to Dusk Competition. He is a Liveryman of the Honourable Company of Air Pilots, a Fellow of the Royal Institute of Navigation and a Member of the Royal Aeronautical Society.

EASA PRIVATE PILOT LICENCE
– AEROPLANE –
PRINCIPLES OF FLIGHT

Before attempting these practice examination papers, you should have read Air Pilot's Manual, Volume 4 – Section 1, Principles of Flight and have completed the Progress Tests throughout the manual.

The Principles of Flight examination consists of 16 questions; the time allowed is 45 minutes.

The pass mark is 75%.

Please read each question carefully and ensure you understand it fully before making your choice of answer.

Each question is multiple choice with four possible answers A, B, C and D. You should indicate your chosen answer by placing a cross in the appropriate box on the answer sheet.

Blank answer sheets are to be found at the end of this publication, these may be photocopied.

INTENTIONALLY BLANK

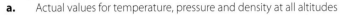

1. The International Standard Atmosphere sets out:

   a. Actual values for temperature, pressure and density at all altitudes
   b. Ambient values for temperature, pressure and density at all altitudes
   c. Theoretical values for temperature, pressure and density at all altitudes
   d. Ambient sea level values for temperature, pressure and density at all altitudes

2. The temperature at 14,000 feet is -9°C. How does this deviate from the ISA temperature?

   a. ISA +6°C
   b. ISA +4°C
   c. ISA -4°C
   d. ISA -6°C

3. The main constituents of the Earth's atmosphere are:

   a. Oxygen, hydrogen and carbon dioxide
   b. Oxygen, nitrogen and water vapour
   c. Carbon dioxide, nitrogen and water vapour
   d. Nitrogen, oxygen and carbon dioxide

4. By volume the ratio of oxygen to nitrogen in the atmosphere is roughly:

   a. 4:1
   b. 3:1
   c. 1:3
   d. 1:4

5. The troposphere is characterised by:

   a. A continuous rise in temperature with increasing height
   b. A continuous reduction in temperature with decreasing height
   c. A continuous reduction in temperature with increasing height
   d. A constant temperature up to the tropopause

6. Air density has a great effect on both airframe and engine performance, which of the following statements is correct?

   a. Density is proportional to pressure and inversely proportional to temperature
   b. Density is proportional to temperature and inversely proportional to pressure
   c. Density is proportional to both temperature and pressure
   d. Density is inversely proportional to both temperature and pressure

7. If the temperature of an airmass remains constant, increasing the pressure will:

   a. Cause the density to increase
   b. Cause the density to decrease
   c. Have no effect on air density
   d. Cause the volume to increase

8. The co-efficient of lift reaches its maximum value at:

   a. An angle of attack of between 5 and 8 degrees
   b. At V_{MD}
   c. At V_{SO}
   d. Just prior to the stalling angle of attack

9. Theoretically, if the angle of attack and other factors remain constant but speed is doubled, the lift created at this higher speed will be:

    (a.) Two times greater than at the lower speed

    c

    b. The same as at the lower speed

    c. Four times greater than at the lower speed

    d. Half as much as at the lower speed

10. Angle of attack may be defined as the angle between:

    a. The chord line of an aerofoil and the horizon

    (b) The chord line of an aerofoil and the relative airflow

    c. The chord line of an aerofoil and the aircraft's longitudinal axis

    d. The chord line of an aerofoil and the aircraft's lateral axis

11. Compared to the free stream airflow, in normal flight air over the top of a wing will:

    a. Decrease in speed

    b. Have the same speed

    (c.) Increase in speed

    d. Have higher pressure

12. Which of the following statements is correct regarding induced drag:

    a. Induced drag increases as airspeed increases

    (b) Induced drag decreases as airspeed increases

    c. Induced drag is unaffected by changes in airspeed

    d. Induced drag decreases as airspeed decreases

13. As angle of attack increases, where will flow separation normally start?

    a. On the lower surface towards the leading edge

    (b.) On the lower surface towards the trailing edge

    c. On the upper surface towards the leading edge

    d. On the upper surface towards the trailing edge

14. A slat will:

    a. Alter the shape (camber) of the aerofoil and lower the angle of attack at which it will stall

    (b) Delay the stall until a higher angle of attack is reached

    c. Enable a steeper approach path to be flow by increase drag

    d. Increase lift by increasing the surface area by extending from the wing's trailing edge

15. In the diagram opposite an aircraft is represented in a balanced level turn. The load factor for this turn is found from:

    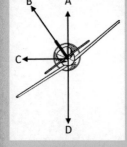

    (a.) $B \div D$

    b. $A \div D$

    c. $B \div C$

    d. $C - A$

16. In a venturi tube

    a. Static pressure increase at the constriction

    b. Dynamic pressure increases as the tube diverges

    (c.) Static pressure reduces at the constriction

    d. Dynamic pressure is lowest within the constriction

END OF PRINCIPLES OF FLIGHT PAPER 1

INTENTIONALLY BLANK

No.	A	B	C	D
1			X	
2		X		
3		X		
4				X
5			X	
6	X			
7	X			
8				X
9			X	
10		X		
11			X	
12		X		
13				X
14		X		
15	X			
16			X	

CORRECT ANSWERS: PERCENTAGES				
12	13	14	15	16
75%	81%	88%	94%	100%

1. **(Answer: C)** The International Standard Atmosphere has been developed by ICAO to describe a theoretical set of atmospheric conditions throughout all levels. The ISA is used as a yardstick with which to compare actual conditions. This is useful to enable aircraft performance to be calculated and instruments calibrated.

    The ISA has mean sea level values of:
    *   Pressure: 1013.2 hPa
    *   Temperature: + 15°C
    *   Density: 1225 g/m³
    *   Lapse Rate: Temperature reducing at 1.98°C per 1000 feet to the tropopause (36,090 feet), above this temperature is assumed to be a constant -56.5°C

    FURTHER READING: APM VOLUME 4, SECTION 3, CHAPTER 25 – PRESSURE INSTRUMENTS (APM2, CHAP.19)

2. **(Answer: B)** For practical purposes the ISA lapse rate of 1.98°C/1000 feet can be rounded up to 2°C/1000 feet.

    The actual temperature given in the question of -9°C is four degrees warmer than the theoretical ISA temperature of -13°C. This is expressed as ISA +4°C.

    14,000 feet ISA TEMPERATURE

    $$= +15 - (2°C \times 14)$$
    $$= +15 -28 = -13°C$$

    ISA LAPSE RATE
    2°C/1000 FEET

    ISA MSL +15°C

    FURTHER READING: APM VOLUME 2, SECTION 2, CHAPTER 16 – THE ATMOSPHERE

3. **(Answer: B)** The main constituent gases within a dry atmosphere are:

    Nitrogen 78%, Oxygen 21% and other gases 1%. In nature there is always some water vapour present up to a maximum of approximately 4%.

    FURTHER READING: APM VOLUME 2, SECTION 2, CHAPTER 16 – THE ATMOSPHERE

4. **(Answer: D)** The main constituent gases within a dry atmosphere are: Nitrogen 78%, Oxygen 21% and other gases 1%. This represents oxygen: nitrogen ratio of 1:4.

    FURTHER READING: APM VOLUME 2, SECTION 2, CHAPTER 16 – THE ATMOSPHERE

5. **(Answer: C)** The troposphere is characterised by a decrease in temperature with increasing height up to the tropopause. Above the tropopause temperature remains constant with further increase in altitude.

    FURTHER READING: APM VOLUME 2, SECTION 2, CHAPTER 16 – THE ATMOSPHERE

6. **(Answer: A)** Density is proportional to pressure, as pressure increases so does density. Conversely if pressure is reduced the air expands and becomes less dense. Density is inversely proportional to temperature, heating an air mass will cause it to expand and reduce its density; in other words as temperature increases, density decreases. Density affects both engine and aerodynamic performance, from the above we can glean that both will be degraded at high altitude (low pressure leading to reduced density) and on hot days (high temperature leading to reduced density).

FURTHER READING: APM VOLUME 2, SECTION 2, CHAPTER 16 – THE ATMOSPHERE

7. **(Answer: A)** Density is proportional to pressure, as pressure increases so does density. If pressure is reduced the air expands and becomes less dense.

FURTHER READING: APM VOLUME 2, SECTION 2, CHAPTER 16 – THE ATMOSPHERE

8. **(Answer: D)** The coefficient of lift is a measure of the amount of lift a wing produces, and is dependent on many factors, namely:
   - wing shape
   - air density
   - speed (squared)
   - wing surface area and
   - angle of attack

   The amount of lift generated by a wing can be calculated using the following formula:
   Lift = Coefficient of Lift x ½ density x velocity squared x wing surface area
   Lift = C_L x ½ρ x V^2 x S
   Plotting angle of attack against coefficient of lift we can see that initially lift increases with increasing angle of attack. At the critical angle (around 16° in a typical training aircraft) there is a sharp drop in the coefficient of lift as the laminar airflow over the wing surface separates and breaks up into eddies, when this happens the wing is said to be stalled. The maximum coefficient of lift occurs just prior to the stall.

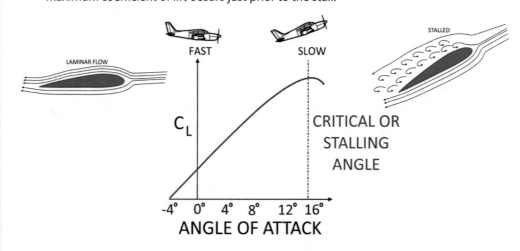

FURTHER READING: APM VOLUME 4, SECTION 1, CHAPTER 3 – AEROFOIL LIFT

9. **(Answer: C)** From the lift equation we can see that lift is proportional to the square of the aircraft's velocity: **Lift = C_L x ½ρ x V^2 x S**

   If the angle of attack and other factors remain constant, an aircraft flying at 200 knots will generate four times the lift that it would do if travelling at 100 knots.

FURTHER READING: APM VOLUME 4, SECTION 1, CHAPTER 3 – AEROFOIL LIFT

10. **(Answer: B)** The angle of attack is the angle between the chord line of an aerofoil and the relative airflow.

    The mean camber line is a line drawn halfway between the upper and lower surfaces of an aerofoil. The chord line is a straight line joining the ends of the mean camber line.

FURTHER READING: APM VOLUME 4, SECTION 1, CHAPTER 3 – AEROFOIL LIFT

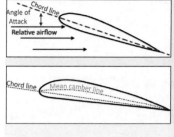

10. ANSWER B

11. **(Answer: C)** Compared to the free stream airflow, in normal flight air over the top of a wing will increase in speed. There are many theories as to exactly how an aerofoil produces lift. The only one we need to be concerned with for now is the "Equal Flow Theory". This theory states that because of an aerofoil's shape the distance air will have to travel is greater over the upper surface than the lower. Airflow over the upper surface will therefore have to accelerate to meet the air flowing below the wing.

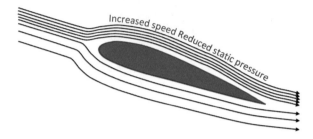

Bernoulli's principle: states that an increase in velocity will lead to a decrease in pressure.

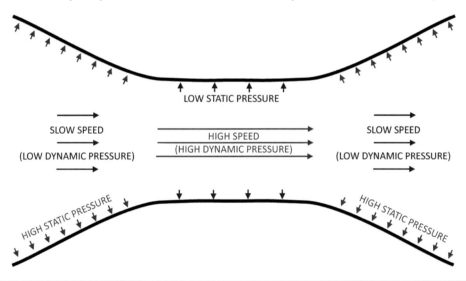

FURTHER READING: APM VOLUME 4, SECTION 1, CHAPTER 3 – AEROFOIL LIFT

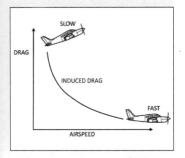

12. ANSWER B

12. **(Answer: B)** Induced drag decreases as airspeed increases. Induced drag is related to angle of attack and is a by-product of lift.

Over most angles of attack there is lower static pressure above a wing than below it; at the wing tip some airflow spills over from the high pressure area under the wing to the low pressure area above creating wing tip vortices. This creates a span-wise movement towards the tip below the wing and towards the fuselage on the upper surface.

The upward motion of the wing tip vortex is outside the span of the wing, however the downward flow is within the span of the wing behind the trailing edge. Additionally there are less powerful trailing edge vortices along the whole wing span. The overall effect is a downwash of air behind the trailing edge.

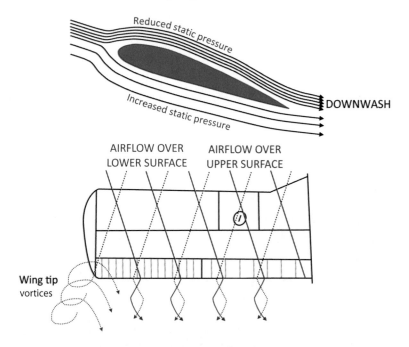

This displacement of air causes a resistance which we call induced drag. The actual amount of induced drag is proportional to the coefficient of lift; the higher the CL the greater the induced drag. The CL also increases with angle of attack and high angles of attack are used at slow speeds and also when manoeuvring.

FURTHER READING: APM VOLUME 4, SECTION 1, CHAPTER 4 – DRAG

13. **(Answer: D)** A wing always stalls at a certain angle of attack, when the laminar flow over the upper surface breaks down. Flow separation will start at the trailing edge and move forwards.

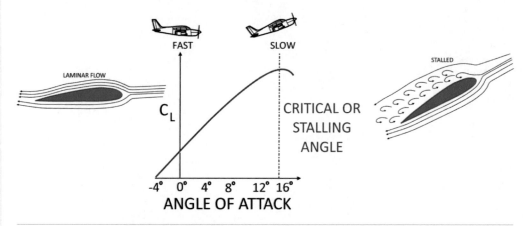

FURTHER READING: APM VOLUME 4, SECTION 1, CHAPTER 14 – STALLING

14. **(Answer: B)** A leading edge slot is a fixed (non-closing) gap behind the wing's leading edge. Air from the high pressure area below the wing can accelerate through the slot towards the low pressure region above the wing. This high-speed flow mixes with and re-energises the boundary layer attached to the upper surface and delays boundary layer separation from the upper surface. Slots naturally exact a penalty on the aircraft in which they are used because they contribute extra drag compared to an unslotted wing. Hence more sophisticated aircraft will have moveable slats on the leading edge, which may be deployed to create a slot when required.

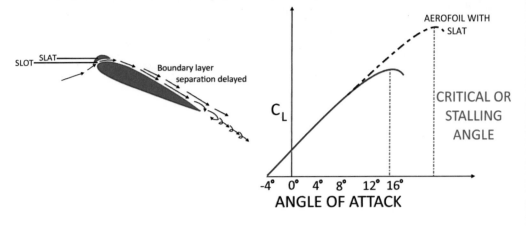

FURTHER READING: APM VOLUME 4, SECTION 1, CHAPTER 9– FLAPS

15. **(Answer: A)** Load factor is defined as the ratio of lift being generated by an aircraft to its weight. Load factor and is normally expressed in terms of "g", because of the relation between load factor and apparent acceleration of gravity felt on board the aircraft. A load factor of one, or 1 g, represents conditions in straight and level flight, where the lift is equal to the weight. Load factors greater or less than one are the result of manoeuvres, turbulence or wind gusts.

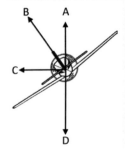

Load factor = L ÷ W
Therefore, in this question it is therefore found from B ÷ D.

FURTHER READING: APM VOLUME 4, SECTION 1, CHAPTER 13 – TURNING

15. ANSWER A

16. **(Answer: C)** Bernoulli's principle: states that an increase in velocity will lead to a decrease in pressure. As air accelerates to go through the constriction the dynamic pressure increases, consequently the static pressure is reduced since the total pressure remains unchanged.

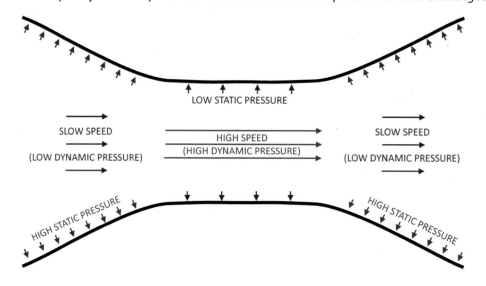

FURTHER READING: APM VOLUME 4, SECTION 1, CHAPTER 3 – AEROFOIL LIFT

END OF EXPLANATIONS PAPER 1

PRINCIPLES OF FLIGHT PAPER 2

1. In flight, an aircraft is said to be in equilibrium when:
    a.   Lift is balanced by drag and weight is balanced by thrust
    b.   Weight is balanced by lift and drag is balanced by thrust
    c.   Weight is balanced by drag and lift is balanced by thrust
    d.   Lift is balanced by thrust and weight is balanced by drag

2. Increasing airspeed will cause:
    a.   Induced drag to increase and parasite drag to decrease
    b.   Induced drag to increase and parasite drag to increase
    c.   Parasite drag to decrease and induced drag to decrease
    d.   Parasite drag to increase and induced drag to decrease

3. In straight and level flight, if the centre of pressure is behind the centre of gravity a ...(i)... couple is produced, requiring the tailplane to produce a ...(ii)... force
    a.   i) nose down   ii) downward
    b.   i) nose down   ii) upward
    c.   i) nose up   ii) downward
    d.   i) nose up   ii) upward

4. Movement of an aeroplane around its lateral axis is called:
    a.   Rolling
    b.   Pitching
    c.   Yawing
    d.   Spinning

5. Movement of an aeroplane around its normal axis is called:
    a.   Rolling
    b.   Pitching
    c.   Yawing
    d.   Spinning

6. The primary effect of aileron input is to create roll, the secondary effect is:
    a.   Yaw followed by spiral dive
    b.   Pitch, from the extra lift generated by the down going wing
    c.   Turn followed by spiral dive
    d.   Bank followed by spiral dive

7. Directional stability is achieved by:
    a.   The tailplane
    b.   The ailerons
    c.   The fin
    d.   The rudder

8. The up-going aileron is rigged to move further than the down-going aileron to counteract:
    a.   Inertia
    b.   Static stability
    c.   Lateral stability
    d.   Adverse aileron yaw

9. The secondary effect of aileron is ... (i)... and the secondary effect of rudder is ...(ii)...:
    a.   i) yaw   ii) roll
    b.   i) roll   ii) yaw
    c.   i) bank   ii) yaw
    d.   i) roll   ii) bank

10. Static stability is an indicator of an aircraft's readiness to:

    a. Continue to diverge from its original position

    b. Return to its original position

    c. Remain at its new position

    d. Oscillate about the original flight path and finally diverge from it

11. Washout on an aircraft's wing is employed to:

    a. Decrease aileron effectiveness

    b. Ensure that the wing tip stalls first

    c. Ensure that the inboard section of the wing stalls first

    d. Ensure the wing stalls evenly along its length

12. A fixed trim tab, or balance tab, on an aileron:

    a. Is adjusted on the ground after a test flight to ensure longitudinally level flight

    b. Is set at the time of manufacture and must not be altered

    c. Is adjusted by the pilot during flight to relieve unwanted control pressures

    d. Is adjusted on the ground after a test flight to ensure laterally level flight

13. An aerofoil reaches maximum aerodynamic efficiency at the point where the lift/drag ratio is at its greatest. For general aviation aircraft this occurs at approximately:

    a. - 5°

    b. 0°

    c. + 4°

    d. + 16 °

14. What effect will extending trailing edge flaps have of the angle of attack at which an aerofoil stalls?

    a. Trailing edge flaps will increase the stalling angle of attack

    b. Trailing edge flaps will have no effect the stalling angle of attack

    c. Trailing edge flaps will either reduce or increase the stalling angle of attack depending on the aircraft's speed

    d. Trailing edge flaps will reduce the stalling angle of attack

15. Ignoring any other factors, should flaps be extended whilst maintaining a constant angle of attack, an aircraft will initially:

    a. Bank

    b. Descend

    c. Yaw

    d. Climb

16. For which part of an aircraft can design have the greatest effect on the induced drag created?

    a. The wing tips

    b. The landing gear

    c. The nose, engine cowling

    d. The aerofoil section

END OF PRINCIPLES OF FLIGHT PAPER 2

INTENTIONALLY BLANK

No.	A	B	C	D
1		X		
2				X
3	X			
4		X		
5			X	
6	X			
7			X	
8				X
9	X			
10		X		
11			X	
12				X
13			X	
14				X
15				X
16	X			

CORRECT ANSWERS:	PERCENTAGES			
12	13	14	15	16
75%	81%	88%	94%	100%

1. **(Answer: B)** For an aircraft in straight and level flight to be in equilibrium lift has to equal weight and thrust must equal drag. In this situation the two couples balance out and there is no resultant force acting on the aircraft.

    Weight – acts vertically downwards and acts through the centre of gravity.

    Lift – is a force which acts upwards at right angles to the relative airflow, it acts through the centre of pressure.

    Thrust – is the forward reaction to air being accelerated backwards by a propeller, it acts through the propeller shaft.

    Drag – acts to oppose the motion of the aircraft and acts parallel to the relative airflow in the opposite direction to the flight path. Any remaining pitching moment is balanced by the tailplane.

    FURTHER READING: APM VOLUME 4, SECTION 1, CHAPTER 7 – STABILITY

2. **(Answer: D)** Increasing airspeed will cause parasite drag to increase and induced drag to decrease.

    Parasite drag – is composed of form drag, interference drag and skin friction, it is proportional to airspeed.

    Induced drag – is a by-product of lift and is proportional to angle of attack. It has more influence at low speed when a high angle of attack is required.

    FURTHER READING: APM VOLUME 4, SECTION 1, CHAPTER 4 – DRAG

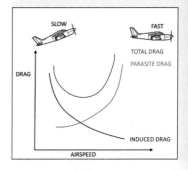

2. ANSWER D

3. **(Answer: A)** In straight and level flight, if the centre of pressure is behind the centre of gravity a nose down couple is produced, requiring the tailplane to produce an aerodynamic downward force.

    FURTHER READING: APM VOLUME 4, SECTION 1, CHAPTER 7 – STABILITY

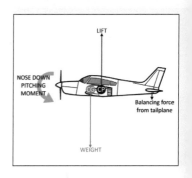

3. ANSWER A

4. **(Answer: B)** The lateral axis runs from one side of the aeroplane to the other passing through the centre of gravity. Movement about the lateral axis is called pitching.

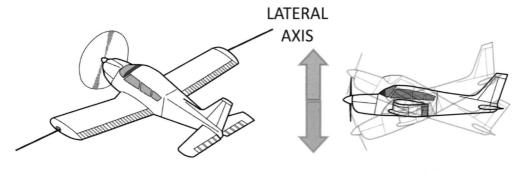

LATERAL AXIS

FURTHER READING: APM VOLUME 4, SECTION 1, CHAPTER 7 – STABILITY

5.   **(Answer: C)** Movement of an aeroplane around its normal axis is called yawing.

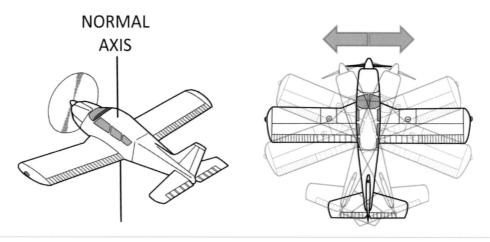

FURTHER READING: APM VOLUME 4, SECTION 1, CHAPTER 7 – STABILITY

6.   **(Answer: A)** The primary effect of aileron input is to create roll. The secondary effect is yaw, which if uncorrected will lead to a spiral dive. Following the initial roll a sideslip force is introduced which acts on the keel surfaces of the aircraft. This happens because the lift vector is tilted into the turn and now has a horizontal component that is not opposed by any other force, the aircraft will therefore slip in that direction. Since there is a larger keel surface behind the centre of gravity than ahead of it, the aircraft's nose will slew in the direction of the sideslip – this motion is yaw towards the lower wing.

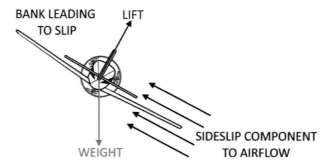

The further effect of yaw is roll, because extra lift is generated from the faster moving outer wing. If not corrected by the pilot his cycle of roll leading to yaw leading to roll will continue and eventually develop into a spiral dive.

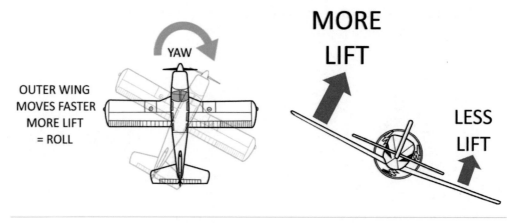

FURTHER READING: APM VOLUME 4, SECTION 1, CHAPTER 7 – STABILITY

7. **(Answer: C)** The fin. Directional stability refers to an aircraft's natural ability to recover from a disturbance in the yawing plane, that is, movement about the normal axis. Should an aircraft be disturbed from its path a sideways motion is introduced. The fin which is a symmetrical aerofoil is now experiencing an angle of attack and will generate a force to restore the nose to its original position.

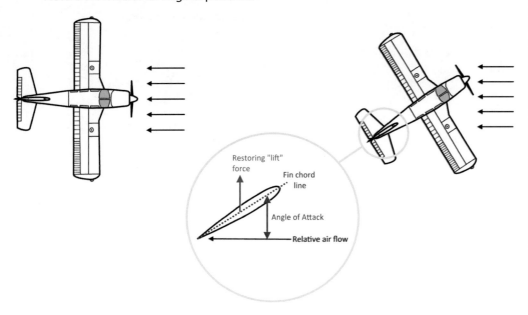

The fin exerts a powerful turning effect as it has a large area and a long moment arm between it and the aircraft's centre of gravity.

FURTHER READING: APM VOLUME 4, SECTION 1, CHAPTER 7 – STABILITY

8. **(Answer: D)** Differential ailerons are designed to minimise adverse aileron yaw. When an aileron is deflected down the effective camber of that wing is increased, also increasing its angle of attack. The lift generated by this wing increases, sadly so does the induced drag. The reverse happens on the wing with the up-going aileron: the effective camber is decreased as is the effective angle of attack, lift decreases and so does drag.

    Lift causes the aircraft to bank in one direction, however the differing drag forces create yaw in the opposite direction.

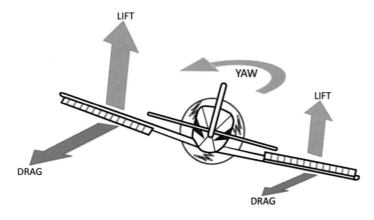

    Differential ailerons increase the drag on the down-going wing, by deflecting the up aileron through a greater angle compared to the down aileron on the up-going wing.

The up aileron generates an increase in profile drag which will tend to yaw the aircraft into the bank. Other methods of reducing adverse aileron yaw are Frise-type aileron (where profile drag is increased on the up-going aileron by projecting its leading edge into the airflow below the wing) or designs coupling the rudder to the ailerons.

FRISE-AILERON

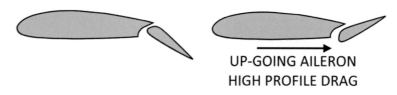

UP-GOING AILERON
HIGH PROFILE DRAG

FURTHER READING: APM VOLUME 4, SECTION 1, CHAPTER 8 – CONTROL

9. **(Answer: A)** The secondary effect of aileron is yaw and the secondary effect of rudder is roll.

Aileron: When aileron is used to roll, the aircraft will adopt a banked attitude, the lift vector now has a horizontal component and the aircraft will tend to side slip towards the lower wing. The side slip causes a relative airflow against the keel surface of the aircraft; there is a larger surface area behind the Centre of Gravity hence the aircraft will turn about its normal axis – yaw. If left uncorrected a spiral dive will develop.

Rudder: As an aircraft yaws the outer wing will move faster and produce more lift than the inner wing giving a tendency to roll towards the inner wing. *See diagram at question 22.*

FURTHER READING: APM VOLUME 4, SECTION 1, CHAPTER 7 – STABILITY

10. **(Answer: B)** Static stability is a measure of how readily an aircraft tends to return to its original condition when disturbed from a condition of steady flight.

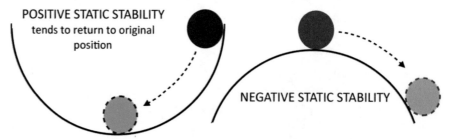

POSITIVE STATIC STABILITY
tends to return to original position

NEGATIVE STATIC STABILITY

Static stability - refers to the aircraft's initial response to a disturbance.

Dynamic stability - refers to the aircraft's subsequent behaviour after the initial static stability response.

FURTHER READING: APM VOLUME 4, SECTION 1, CHAPTER 7 – STABILITY

11. **(Answer: C)** Washout is a reduction in the angle of incidence (and consequently the angle of attack) from wing root to wing tip. The angle of incidence is set by the aircraft designer and describes the angle subtended by the wing chord and the aircraft's longitudinal axis.

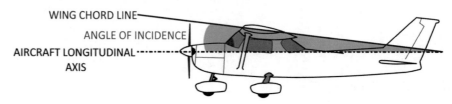

WING CHORD LINE
ANGLE OF INCIDENCE
AIRCRAFT LONGITUDINAL AXIS

Since a wing will stall at a particular angle of attack washout ensures that any stall will begin at the root. It is undesirable for the wing tip to stall first as any use of aileron when approaching the critical angle could induce yaw and lead to an incipient spin; with the stall starting at the root, controllability, though reduced, can be maintained.

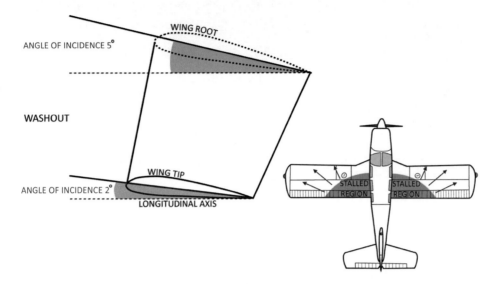

An additional benefit to washout is that there is a lesser pressure difference between the lower and upper surfaces at the tip meaning reduced wing tip vortices and lower induced drag.

FURTHER READING: APM VOLUME 4, SECTION 1, CHAPTER 4 & 14 – DRAG & STALLING

12. **(Answer: D)** A fixed trim or balanced tab is a small flexible metal tab affixed to the rear of a control surface. If an aircraft exhibits a consistent fault when flying, for example flying with one wing low, the tab can be bent to alter forces on the control surface. Any adjustments can only be done on the ground and the efficacy of the alteration established by a test flight. Essentially corrections to a fixed tab will involve a series of trial and error adjustments and test flights.

FURTHER READING: APM VOLUME 4, SECTION 1, CHAPTER 8 – CONTROL

13. **(Answer: C)** The lift/drag ratio defines the proportion of lift to drag at different angles of attack. For a typical general aviation aircraft the maximum L/D ratio is reached at an angle of attack of approximately +4°.

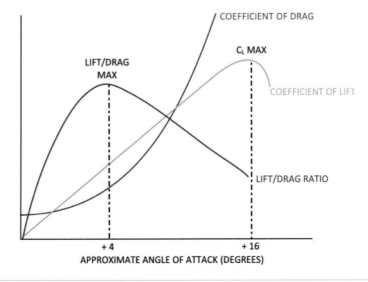

FURTHER READING: APM VOLUME 4, SECTION 1, CHAPTER 5 – LIFT/DRAG RATIO

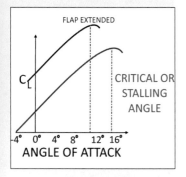

14 & 15. ANSWER D

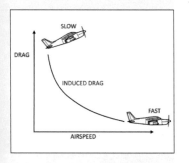

16. ANSWER B

14. **(Answer: D)** When compared to the chord line of a clean aerofoil, extending trailing edge flaps will give a lower stalling angle of attack. Extending flaps increases the camber of the wing aerofoil, thus raising the maximum lift coefficient. This increase in maximum lift coefficient allows the aircraft to generate a given amount of lift with a slower speed. Therefore, extending the flaps reduces the stalling speed of the aircraft, but will lower the critical angle.

FURTHER READING: APM VOLUME 4, SECTION 1, CHAPTER 14 – STALLING

15. **(Answer: D)** Climb. Extending flaps increases the camber of the wing aerofoil, thus raising the maximum lift coefficient.

Maintaining a constant angle of attack and making no other changes, the extra lift generated from flap extension will exceed the weight of the aircraft by a greater margin and lead to the aircraft gaining altitude.

FURTHER READING: APM VOLUME 4, SECTION 1, CHAPTER 14 – STALLING

16. **(Answer: A)** The wing tip design will have the greatest effect on induced drag.

Induced drag decreases as airspeed increases, is related to angle of attack and is an unavoidable by-product when generating lift from a wing.

Over most angles of attack there is lower static pressure above a wing than below it; at the wing tip some airflow spills over from the high pressure area under the wing to the low pressure area above creating wing tip vortices. This creates a span-wise movement towards the tip below the wing and towards the fuselage on the upper surface. The upward motion of the wing tip vortex is outside the span of the wing, however the downward flow is within the span of the wing behind the trailing edge.

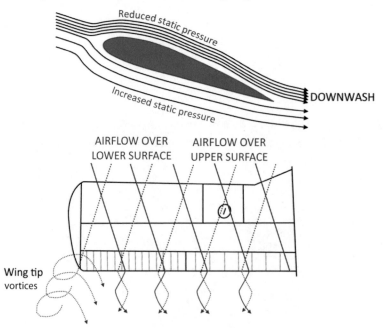

It is possible, through design, to reduce the extent of wing tip vortices. For example, gliders are designed to have long, narrow wings (a high aspect ratio) which lessen induced drag or modern airliners which employ "winglets" at the wing tips to reduce the energy in the circular airflow of the vortex.

FURTHER READING: APM VOLUME 4, SECTION 1, CHAPTER 4 – DRAG

END OF EXPLANATIONS PAPER 2

1. An anti-balance tab is fitted to a control surface to:

    a. Aid the pilot in moving the control surface at high speed
    b. Aid the movement of the control column
    c. Ensure that control column loads increase with increased deflection of the control surface
    d. Control the position of the centre of pressure on the control surface

2. Following a disturbance from a stable trimmed position, an aircraft with neutral stability will:

    a. Return to its original attitude
    b. Continue to diverge from its original attitude
    c. Remain in its new attitude
    d. Return to its original attitude, overshoot but eventually return to its original attitude

3. Using small flap settings during take-off:

    a. Gives a shorter take-off ground run
    b. Improves the initial rate of climb
    c. Gives a steeper climb angle
    d. Gives a longer take-off ground run

4. When compared to the chord line of a clean aerofoil, extending trailing edge flaps will give:

    a. A lower stalling angle of attack
    b. A higher stalling angle of attack
    c. No change in the critical angle
    d. A higher angle of incidence

5. Slots increase the stalling angle of attack by:

    a. Providing extra lift from the leading edge
    b. Increasing the effective wing area
    c. Changing the camber of the wing
    d. Delaying the breakup of laminar air flow over the upper surface

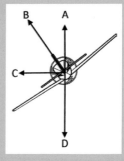

6. The illustration right depicts an aircraft in a balanced level turn to port. Lift is represented by vector:

    a. D
    b. C
    c. B
    d. A

7. Some control surfaces have a tendency to "flutter" at high speed, this can be avoided:

    a. With the use of a balance tab
    b. With the use of a mass balance
    c. With the use of an anti-balance tab
    d. With the use of a spring tab

8. The basic stall speed of an aircraft is 80 knots. In a level turn with a 60° angle of bank, the same aircraft will have a stalling speed of:

    a. 195 knots
    b. 103 knots
    c. 121 knots
    d. 113 knots

9. Should the centre of gravity be at or close to its aft limit one effect will be:

    a. An increase in longitudinal stability
    b. The stalling speed will increase
    c. A reduction in elevator force required during the flare
    d. An increase in elevator force required during the flare

10. With a simple trim tab set during flight, any movement of the associated control surface will cause the tab to:

    a. Move in the opposite direction to the control surface
    b. Move in the same direction as the control surface and will need to be re-set
    c. Remain in a constant position relative to the control surface
    d. Remain in a constant position relative to the airflow

11. Should the centre of gravity be at or close to its forward limit one effect will be:

    a. A decrease in longitudinal stability
    b. A requirement for high elevator forces during the flare
    c. A reduction in the stalling speed
    d. A reduction in elevator force required during the flare

12. An aircraft wing will stall at a particular...(i)... The onset of a stall is characterised by a ...(ii)... attitude and ...(iii)...

    a. i) airspeed   ii) pitch up   iii) the aircraft sinking
    b. i) angle of incidence   ii) pitch down   iii) a wing drop
    c. i) airspeed   ii) pitch down   iii) a wing drop
    d. i) angle of attack   ii) pitch down   iii) the aircraft sinking

13. According to EASA Certification Specifications, in a clean configuration the positive limit manoeuvring load factor for a general aviation aircraft in the utility category, may not be less than:

    a. 2.2
    b. 3.8
    c. 4.4
    d. 5.8

14. An aircraft having a lift/drag ratio of 8:1 will have what still air gliding range from 4,000 feet above ground level?

    a. 6.1 nm
    b. 5.3 nm
    c. 5.0 nm
    d. 0.66 nm

15. An aircraft having a lift/drag ratio of 9:1 will have what still air gliding range from 5,000 feet above ground level?

    a. 7.5 nm
    b. 6.9 nm
    c. 0.83 nm
    d. 7.1 nm

16. As angle of attack increases, the stagnation point will move .... (1) .... and the area of lowest pressure will move .... (2) ....

    a. 1. Down the trailing edge 2. Forwards
    b. 1. Up the leading edge 2. Aft
    c. 1. Down the leading edge 2. Aft
    d. 1. Down the leading edge 2. Forwards

INTENTIONALLY BLANK

No.	A	B	C	D
1			X	
2			X	
3	X			
4	X			
5				X
6			X	
7		X		
8				X
9			X	
10			X	
11		X		
12				X
13			X	
14		X		
15	X			
16				X

CORRECT ANSWERS: PERCENTAGES				
12	13	14	15	16
75%	81%	88%	94%	100%

1. **(Answer: C)** An anti-balance tab moves in the same direction as the control surface to which it is attached. It will make movement of the control surface more difficult and require more force to be applied to the control column by the pilot. This may seem counter-intuitive, but it is commonly used on aircraft where it is desirable to prevent pilots from moving the surface too far and over-controlling or where the aircraft requires additional stability in that particular axis of movement. The anti-balance tab serves artificially to increase stability and also makes the controls heavier in feel to the pilot.

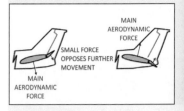

1. ANSWER C

Anti-balance tabs are often fitted to horizontal stabilators where, because of their large area, small control inputs can generate large aerodynamic forces.

FURTHER READING: APM VOLUME 4, SECTION 1, CHAPTER 8 – CONTROL

2. **(Answer: C)** Following a disturbance from a stable trimmed position, an aircraft with neutral stability will remain in its new attitude.

FURTHER READING: APM VOLUME 4, SECTION 1, CHAPTER 7 – STABILITY

3. **(Answer: A)** Using small flap settings (up to approximately 20°) during take-off decreases the ground run required. If a large flap setting is used drag will greatly increase and no benefit will be gained; small settings, however, will lower the stalling speed enabling both the lift-off and take-off safety speeds to be reduced. Consequently the aircraft will reach its lift-off speed after a shorter ground roll, meaning that shorter runways can be used or runways with a poor surface can be left behind more quickly!

Though the ground run is reduced due to the increased lift generated by the use of flap, the initial rate and angle of climb will both be reduced due to the increase in drag. Although small flap settings do have a drag penalty, generally speaking it is relatively small. Large flap settings (the last stage) add little lift, but do add a large amount of drag. The use of this setting on take off would reduce acceleration and significantly degrade climb performance; hence their use is restricted to landing.

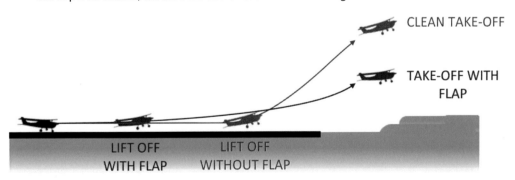

CLEAN TAKE-OFF

TAKE-OFF WITH FLAP

LIFT OFF WITH FLAP

LIFT OFF WITHOUT FLAP

FURTHER READING: APM VOLUME 4, SECTION 1, CHAPTER 9– FLAPS

4. **(Answer: A)** When compared to the chord line of a clean aerofoil, extending trailing edge flaps will give a lower stalling angle of attack. Extending flaps increases the camber of the wing aerofoil, thus raising the maximum lift coefficient. This increase in maximum lift coefficient allows the aircraft to generate a given amount of lift with a slower speed. Therefore, extending the flaps reduces the stalling speed of the aircraft, but will lower the critical angle.

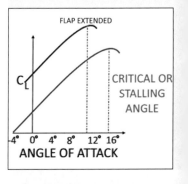

4. ANSWER A

FURTHER READING: APM VOLUME 4, SECTION 1, CHAPTER 9– FLAPS

5. **(Answer: D)** A leading edge slot is a fixed (non-closing) gap behind the wing's leading edge. Air from the high pressure area below the wing can accelerate through the slot towards the low pressure region above the wing. This high-speed flow mixes with and re-energises the boundary layer attached to the upper surface and delays boundary layer separation from the upper surface. Slots naturally exact a penalty on the aircraft in which they are used because they contribute extra drag compared to an unslotted wing. Hence more sophisticated aircraft will have moveable slats on the leading edge, which may be deployed to create a slot when required.

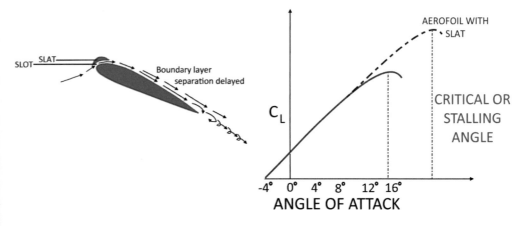

FURTHER READING: APM VOLUME 4, SECTION 1, CHAPTER 9– FLAPS

6. **(Answer: C)** Lift is represented by vector B. A represents the vertical component of lift and C the horizontal component of lift in the turn.

FURTHER READING: APM VOLUME 4, SECTION 1, CHAPTER 13 – TURNING

7. **(Answer: B)** Some control surfaces have a tendency to "flutter" when operating in the higher speed range as a result of changes in pressure distribution over the surface with changes in angle of attack. Flutter can cause serious oscillations to develop and to prevent it aircraft designers must alter the mass distribution of the surface. A mass balance will achieve this, and is placed forward of the hinge line in order to move the centre of gravity of the surface forward. *See diagram on page 36 (Paper 4, Explanation 5).*

FURTHER READING: APM VOLUME 4, SECTION 1, CHAPTER 8 – CONTROL

8. **(Answer: D)** In a 60° bank the load factor is 2. At 2g the stall speed increases by $\sqrt{2}$ which is 1.41. Equating to 41% increase in stall speed.

    Basic stalling speed = 80 knots
    41% of 80 = 80 x $\frac{41}{100}$ = 32.8
    Stalling speed at 60° bank = 80 + 32.8 = 112.8 knots

FURTHER READING: APM VOLUME 4, SECTION 1, CHAPTER 14 – STALLING

9. **(Answer: C)** If the centre of gravity is at or close to its aft limit the aircraft's longitudinal stability is reduced, i.e. it becomes less stable in pitch. With an aft C of G lift generated from the wing will give a nose-up pitching moment, even a slight increase in angle of attack will cause the lift to increase and a greater nose-up pitching moment to be experienced. With an aft C of G it is the aircraft's natural tendency to pitch up meaning that only very slight elevator forces will be required in the flare. The danger here would be to over pitch and stall onto the runway.

FURTHER READING: APM VOLUME 4, SECTION 1, CHAPTER 7 – STABILITY

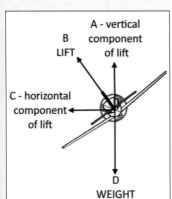

6. ANSWER C

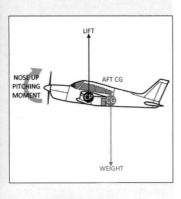

9. ANSWER C

10. **(Answer: C)** Once the trim tab has been set, any subsequent movement of the associated control surface by the pilot will not affect the trim tab. With respect to the control surface the tab will remain in the same position until the pilot decides to re-trim.

FURTHER READING: APM VOLUME 4, SECTION 1, CHAPTER 8 – CONTROL

11. **(Answer: B)** If the centre of gravity is at or close to its forward limit the aircraft's longitudinal stability is increased, i.e. it becomes more stable in pitch. The aircraft will feel extremely nose heavy and resistant to changes in pitch. It is probable that the pilot may not be able to prevent the nose pitching down at low speed, for instance when landing, even with the control column fully aft.

FURTHER READING: APM VOLUME 4, SECTION 1, CHAPTER 7 – STABILITY

12. **(Answer: D)** An aircraft wing will stall at a particular angle of attack. The onset of a stall is characterised by a pitch down attitude and the aircraft sinking.

FURTHER READING: APM VOLUME 4, SECTION 1, CHAPTER 14 – STALLING

13. **(Answer: C)** The positive limit manoeuvring load factor for a general aviation aircraft in the utility category may not be less than 4.4 g. EASA CS 23.337

Load factor is defined as the ratio of lift to weight. Load factor and is normally expressed in terms of "g", because of the relation between load factor and apparent acceleration of gravity felt on board the aircraft. A load factor of one, or 1 g, represents conditions in straight and level flight, where the lift is equal to the weight. Load factors greater or less than one are the result of manoeuvres, turbulence or wind gusts.

Exceeding either positive or negative load factor limits must be avoided because of the possibility of exceeding the structural load limits of the airplane.

FURTHER READING: APM VOLUME 4, SECTION 1, CHAPTER 14 – STALLING

14. **(Answer: B)** 5.3 nm. The lift/drag ratio equates to the glide ratio when flown at a constant speed. The glide ratio tells us the ratio between the change in forward distance travelled and the change in height lost. In this case 8:1 is telling us that for every 8 units the aircraft travels forward it will lose 1 unit of height.

To find how far the aircraft in this question will glide it is first necessary convert the height in feet to nm. There are roughly 6,076 feet in 1 nm : 4,000 ÷ 6,076 = 0.658 nm.

0.658 nm is therefore the height available to lose and to find how far the aircraft will travel forward in that time multiply by the "lift" part from the L/D ratio:

0.658 x 8 = 5.26 nm

Closest answer 5.3 nm

FURTHER READING: APM VOLUME 4, SECTION 1, CHAPTER 5 – LIFT/DRAG RATIO

15. **(Answer: A)** 7.5 nm. The lift/drag ratio equates to the glide ratio when flown at a constant speed. The glide ratio tells us the ratio between the change in forward distance travelled and the change in height lost. In this case 9:1 is telling us that for every 9 units the aircraft travels forward it will lose 1 unit of height.

To find how far the aircraft in this question will glide it is first necessary convert the height in feet to nm. There are roughly 6,076 feet in 1 nm : 5,000 ÷ 6,076 = 0.83 nm.

0.83 nm is therefore the height available to lose and to find how far the aircraft will travel forward in that time multiply by the "lift" part from the L/D ratio:

0.83 x 9 = 7.5 nm

FURTHER READING: APM VOLUME 4, SECTION 1, CHAPTER 5 – LIFT/DRAG RATIO

16. **(Answer: D)** The stagnation point is where the airflow comes to a halt and separates into a flow over the upper surface and a flow below the wing. As angle of attack increases the stagnation point will move down the leading edge of the wing, at the same time the area of lowest pressure will move forward.

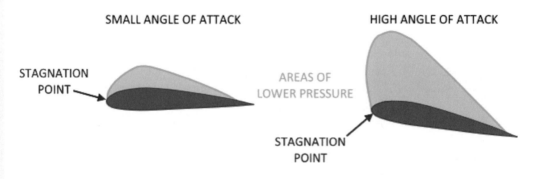

SMALL ANGLE OF ATTACK   HIGH ANGLE OF ATTACK

STAGNATION POINT   AREAS OF LOWER PRESSURE

STAGNATION POINT

FURTHER READING: APM VOLUME 4, SECTION 1, CHAPTER 3 – AEROFOIL LIFT

END OF EXPLANATIONS PAPER 3

1. Which of the following statements is correct regarding parasite drag:

   a. Parasite drag increases as airspeed increases

   b. Parasite drag decreases as airspeed increases

   c. Parasite drag is unaffected by changes in airspeed

   d. Parasite drag decreases as airspeed decreases

2. In relation to drag which of the following statements is correct?

   a. Speed has no effect on drag

   b. Parasite drag has more influence at low speeds; induced drag has more influence at high speed

   c. Both parasite and induced drag increase with increasing speed

   d. Induced drag has more influence at low speeds; parasite drag has more influence at high speed

3. Maintaining a constant angle of attack and increasing airspeed will cause:

   a. Lift and drag to decrease

   b. Lift to increase and drag to decrease

   c. Lift to decrease and drag to increase

   d. Lift and drag to increase

4. Compared to the free stream flow, in normal flight air pressure under a wing will be:

   a. Lower

   b. Higher

   c. The same

   d. Initially higher, then lower

5. On a control surface a "Mass Balance":

   a. Moves the surface's centre of gravity aft

   b. Prevents flutter at high speed

   c. Makes it easier for the pilot to move the control surface

   d. Provides resistance, making it more difficult for the pilot to move the control surface

6. Following a disturbance, an aircraft which returns to its original flight path without the pilot taking any corrective action is said to have:

   a. Stability

   b. Instability

   c. Neutral stability

   d. Neutral instability

7. A wing stalls at:

   a. A given speed

   b. A given angle of incidence

   c. A given angle of attack

   d. A given weight

8. At a given constant weight the stall speed of an aircraft is proportional to the:

   a. Square of the aircraft's weight

   b. Square root of the load factor

   c. Square of the load factor

   d. Square of the aircraft's weight

9. Leading edge slots increase the stalling, or critical angle, of a wing by:

    a. Delaying the breakup of laminar air flow over the upper surface
    b. Increasing the effective wing area
    c. Changing the camber of the wing
    d. Providing extra lift from the leading edge

10. The temperature at 11,000 feet is -2°C. How does this deviate from the ISA temperature?

    a. ISA + 3°C
    b. ISA - 7°C
    c. ISA +7°C
    d. ISA +5°C

11. A parcel of saturated air, when compared to a parcel of dry air at the same temperature and pressure will be:

    a. Less dense
    b. More dense
    c. Of exactly the same density
    d. Twice the volume

12. The basic stall speed of an aircraft is 60 knots. In a level turn with a 60° angle of bank, the same aircraft will have a stalling speed of:

    a. 101 knots
    b. 85 knots
    c. 146 knots
    d. 95 knots

13. With regards to the forces acting upon an aircraft in flight. In a steady straight climb:

    a. Thrust is greater than drag, lift is greater than weight
    b. Thrust is greater than drag, lift is less than weight
    c. Thrust is greater than drag, lift is equal to weight
    d. Thrust is equal to drag, lift is equal to weight

14. In nil wind, the maximum glide distance will be achieved fly flying at what speed?

    a. Just above the stall speed
    b. The speed giving the minimum L:D ratio
    c. The speed giving minimum drag
    d. The speed giving the maximum drag

15. To provide an efficient angle of attack throughout the full length of the blade, the blade angle is:

    a. Progressively reduced from hub to tip
    b. Progressively increased from hub to tip
    c. Constant along the length of the blade
    d. Constant to 60% of the blade then reduces to the tip

16. The maximum speed at which a full application of a primary flight control will not overstress the airframe is known as:

    a. V_{MD}
    b. V_{FE}
    c. V_{NE}
    d. V_{A}

END OF PRINCIPLES OF FLIGHT PAPER 4

INTENTIONALLY BLANK

No.	A	B	C	D
1	X			
2				X
3				X
4		X		
5		X		
6	X			
7			X	
8		X		
9	X			
10				X
11	X			
12		X		
13		X		
14			X	
15	X			
16				X

CORRECT ANSWERS:	PERCENTAGES			
12	13	14	15	16
75%	81%	88%	94%	100%

1. **(Answer: A)** Parasite drag increases as airspeed increases.

   Parasite drag is composed of:
   Skin friction – the friction force between the aircraft and the air through which it is moving.

   Form drag – the resistance caused by moving an object through the air. The larger the object the larger the "form" presented to the airflow. The key to minimising form drag is to streamline the object concerned.

   Interference drag – due to airflow "interference" at the junctions between the various parts of the aircraft; for example between the wing and fuselage, tail and fuselage, etc...With zero airspeed there is no relative motion between the aircraft and the air flow, therefore there is no parasite drag. With an increase in airspeed skin friction, form drag and interference drag all increase. Doubling the airspeed will give four times the parasite drag.

   Drag = C_D x ½ρ x V^2 x S

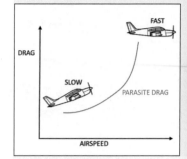

1. ANSWER A

FURTHER READING: APM VOLUME 4, SECTION 1, CHAPTER 4 – DRAG

2. **(Answer: D)** Induced drag has more influence at low speeds (high angles of attack); parasite drag has more influence at high speed.

FURTHER READING: APM VOLUME 4, SECTION 1, CHAPTER 4 – DRAG

3. **(Answer: D)** Maintaining a constant angle of attack and increasing airspeed will cause an increase in both lift and drag. Lift and drag are both proportional to the square of speed, at high speed total drag is almost entirely due to parasite drag *(induced drag is virtually nil).*

   Lift = C_L x ½ρ x V^2 x S

   Drag = C_D x ½ρ X V^2 x S

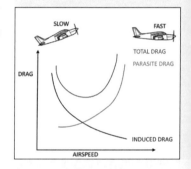

2. ANSWER D

FURTHER READING: APM VOLUME 4, SECTION 1, CHAPTER 4 – DRAG

4. **(Answer: B)** Compared to the free stream flow, in normal flight air pressure under a wing will be higher.

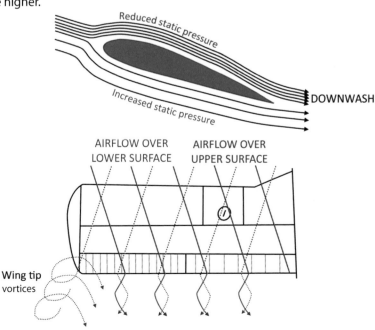

Reduced static pressure

Increased static pressure

DOWNWASH

AIRFLOW OVER LOWER SURFACE   AIRFLOW OVER UPPER SURFACE

Wing tip vortices

FURTHER READING: APM VOLUME 4, SECTION 1, CHAPTER 4 – DRAG

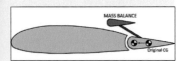

5. ANSWER B

5. **(Answer: B)** Some control surfaces have a tendency to "flutter" when operating in the higher speed range as a result of changes in pressure distribution over the surface with angle of attack changes. Flutter can cause serious oscillations to develop and to prevent it aircraft designers must alter the mass distribution of the surface. A mass balance will achieve this and is placed forward of the hinge line in order to move the centre of gravity of the surface forward.

FURTHER READING: APM VOLUME 4, SECTION 1, CHAPTER 8 – CONTROL

6. **(Answer: A)** Following a disturbance, an aircraft which returns to its original flight path without the pilot taking any corrective action is said to have positive stability.

Static stability - refers to the aircraft's initial response to a disturbance.

Dynamic stability - refers to the aircraft's subsequent behaviour after the initial static stability response. *Stability may be further classified as follows:*

Positive stability - the aircraft tends to return to original condition after a disturbance.

Negative stability - the aircraft tends to increase the disturbance.

Neutral stability - the aircraft remains at the new condition.

Positive Dynamic Stability

Negative Dynamic Stability

Neutral Dynamic Stability

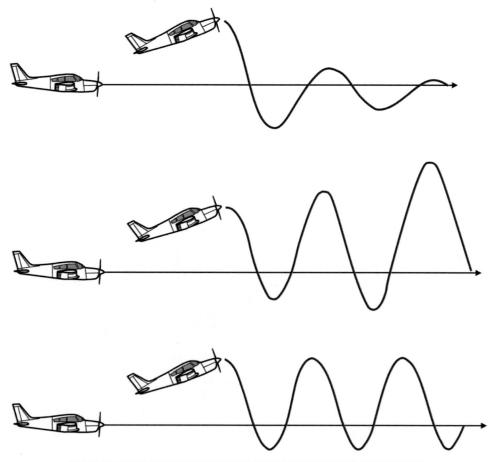

ALL THE AIRCRAFT BELOW POSSESS POSITIVE STATIC STABILITY:
The initial tendency is to return to the original position

FURTHER READING: APM VOLUME 4, SECTION 1, CHAPTER 7 – STABILITY

7.   **(Answer: C)** A wing always stalls at a given angle of attack, the critical angle.

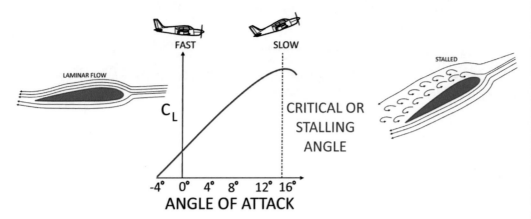

The speed at which the stall will occur varies according to the:

- **Lift produced by the aerofoil** – any manoeuvre that requires extra lift (e.g. turning) will increase the stalling speed.
- **Aircraft's weight** – stalling speed will increase with increase in weight.
- **Load factor** – stall speed increases with load factor
- **Power** – approaching the stall a vertical component of thrust can support some weight, leading to a lower stall speed
- **Bank angle** – increases load factor. In a 60° bank you will experience 2g. The stall speed will increase by $\sqrt{2}$ (which equates to around a 41% increase)
- **Flap selection** – use of flap lowers the stall speed, as the aerofoil will have a higher $C_L$max

FURTHER READING: APM VOLUME 4, SECTION 1, CHAPTER 14 – STALLING

8.   **(Answer: B)** At a given constant weight the stall speed of an aircraft is proportional to the square root of the load factor. Any situation that requires more lift to be generated by the wings will increase the load factor and consequently the stalling speed.

Load factor is traditionally referred to as g, because of the relation between load factor and apparent acceleration of gravity felt on board the aircraft. A load factor of one, or 1 g, represents conditions in straight and level flight, where the lift is equal to the weight. Load factors greater or less than one are the result of manoeuvres, turbulence or wind gusts. At 2g the stall speed increases by $\sqrt{2}$ = 1.41. Equating to 41% increase in stall speed. At 3g the stall speed increases by $\sqrt{3}$ = 1.73. Equating to 73% increase in stall speed.

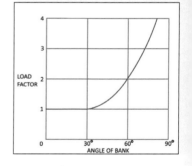

8. ANSWER B

FURTHER READING: APM VOLUME 4, SECTION 1, CHAPTER 14 – STALLING

9.   **(Answer: A)** A leading edge slot is a fixed (non-closing) gap behind the wing's leading edge. Air from the high pressure area below the wing can accelerate through the slot towards the low pressure region above the wing. This high-speed flow mixes with and re-energises the boundary layer attached to the upper surface and delays boundary layer separation from the upper surface.

Slots naturally exact a penalty on the aircraft in which they are used because they contribute extra drag compared to an unslotted wing. Hence more sophisticated aircraft will have moveable slots on the leading edge, which may be deployed to create a slot when required. *See diagram with question 5 on page 29.*

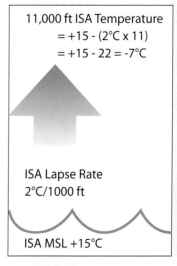

11,000 ft ISA Temperature
= +15 - (2°C x 11)
= +15 - 22 = -7°C

ISA Lapse Rate
2°C/1000 ft

ISA MSL +15°C

FURTHER READING: APM VOLUME 4, SECTION 1, CHAPTER 14 – STALLING

10.   **(Answer: D)** The temperature at 11,000 feet is -2°C, 5 degrees warmer than the theoretical ISA temperature of -7°C. The atmosphere is ISA +5°C.

10. ANSWER D

FURTHER READING: APM VOLUME 2, SECTION 2, CHAPTER 16 – THE ATMOSPHERE

11. **(Answer: A)** Water vapour is lighter than other atmospheric gases, moist air is therefore less dense than dry air. (Molecular masses: $N_2 = 28$, $O_2 = 30$, $H_2O = 17$)

FURTHER READING: APM VOLUME 2, SECTION 2, CHAPTER 16 – THE ATMOSPHERE

12. **(Answer: B)** In a 60° bank the load factor is 2. At 2g the stall speed increases by $\sqrt{2}$ which is 1.41. Equating to 41% increase in stall speed.

Basic stalling speed = 60 knots
41% of 60 = 60 x $\frac{41}{100}$ = 24.6
Stalling speed at 60° bank = 60 + 24.6 = 84.6 knots

FURTHER READING: APM VOLUME 4, SECTION 1, CHAPTER 14 – STALLING

13. **(Answer: B)** In a steady straight climb thrust is greater than drag, lift is less than weight. In straight and level flight thrust opposes drag and lift opposes weight. In a climb excess thrust is required, thrust must still balance drag but now a vertical component of thrust is required to support some of the aircraft's weight; the lift generated by the wings supports the remainder of the weight. Therefore lift in a climb is actually less than weight.

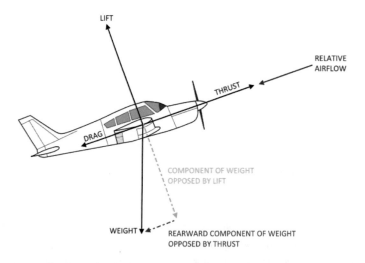

FURTHER READING: APM VOLUME 4, SECTION 1, CHAPTER 10 – STRAIGHT & LEVEL

14. **(Answer: C)** Assuming no wind, the maximum glide distance will be achieved fly flying at the speed which gives minimum drag.

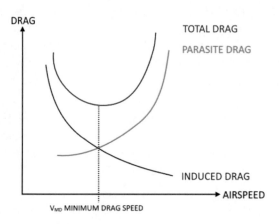

FURTHER READING: APM VOLUME 4, SECTION 1, CHAPTER 4 – DRAG

15. **(Answer: A)** Ideally a propeller should produce uniform thrust along the length of the blade. Therefore the blade is twisted so that the blade angle, and hence the angle of attack, reduces from hub to tip. The result is that the faster moving parts of the propeller have a smaller angle of attack and the slower segments have a larger angle of attack, hence overall the thrust is even along the length of the blade.

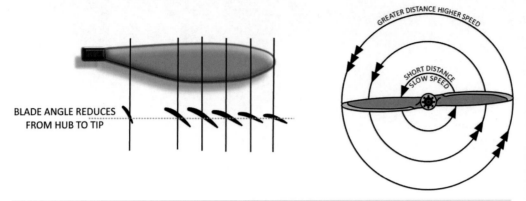

BLADE ANGLE REDUCES
FROM HUB TO TIP

GREATER DISTANCE HIGHER SPEED

SHORT DISTANCE
SLOW SPEED

FURTHER READING: APM VOLUME 4, SECTION 1, CHAPTER 6 – THRUST FROM THE PROPELLER
---

16. **(Answer: D)** V_A is the design manoeuvre speed; above this speed the full application of any flight control may generate a force greater than the aircraft's structural limitations.

FURTHER READING: APM VOLUME 4, SECTION 4, CHAPTER 29 – AIRFRAME LIMITATIONS

END OF EXPLANATIONS PAPER 4

INTENTIONALLY BLANK

Blank Answer Sheets   43 - 46

INTENTIONALLY BLANK

ANSWER SHEETS

PAPER NO.				
	A	B	C	D
1				
2				
3				
4				
5				
6				
7				
8				
9				
10				
11				
12				
13				
14				
15				
16				

PAPER NO.				
	A	B	C	D
1				
2				
3				
4				
5				
6				
7				
8				
9				
10				
11				
12				
13				
14				
15				
16				

PAPER NO.				
	A	B	C	D
1				
2				
3				
4				
5				
6				
7				
8				
9				
10				
11				
12				
13				
14				
15				
16				

PAPER NO.				
	A	B	C	D
1				
2				
3				
4				
5				
6				
7				
8				
9				
10				
11				
12				
13				
14				
15				
16				

PAPER NO.				
	A	B	C	D
1				
2				
3				
4				
5				
6				
7				
8				
9				
10				
11				
12				
13				
14				
15				
16				

PAPER NO.				
	A	B	C	D
1				
2				
3				
4				
5				
6				
7				
8				
9				
10				
11				
12				
13				
14				
15				
16				

PAPER NO.				
	A	B	C	D
1				
2				
3				
4				
5				
6				
7				
8				
9				
10				
11				
12				
13				
14				
15				
16				

PAPER NO.				
	A	B	C	D
1				
2				
3				
4				
5				
6				
7				
8				
9				
10				
11				
12				
13				
14				
15				
16				

PAPER NO.				
	A	B	C	D
1				
2				
3				
4				
5				
6				
7				
8				
9				
10				
11				
12				
13				
14				
15				
16				

PAPER NO.				
	A	B	C	D
1				
2				
3				
4				
5				
6				
7				
8				
9				
10				
11				
12				
13				
14				
15				
16				

PAPER NO.				
	A	B	C	D
1				
2				
3				
4				
5				
6				
7				
8				
9				
10				
11				
12				
13				
14				
15				
16				

PAPER NO.				
	A	B	C	D
1				
2				
3				
4				
5				
6				
7				
8				
9				
10				
11				
12				
13				
14				
15				
16				